The W... ...est

WACKY ONE-LINE JOKES

Bob Phillips

HARVEST HOUSE PUBLISHERS

EUGENE, OREGON

THE WORLD'S GREATEST WACKY ONE-LINE JOKES

Copyright © 2005 by Bob Phillips
Published by Harvest House Publishers
Eugene, Oregon 97402

ISBN 0-7369-1426-9

Printed in the United States of America

05 06 07 08 09 10 11 12 / BC-CF / 12 11 10 9 8 7 6 5 4 3 2 1

Accidents

There would be far fewer accidents if we could only teach telephone poles to be more careful.

Aches and Pains

I've got so many aches and pains right now that a new one will have to wait about a week before I can feel it.

Actor

An actor is a man with an infinite capacity for taking praise.

Actress

The girl who has half a mind to become an actress doesn't realize that that's all it requires.

Adam and Eve

What Adam and Eve started, atom and evil may end.

Advice

We always admire the intelligence of those who ask us for advice.

Perhaps one of the reasons why we get so much free advice is that it's easier than helping.

Advice is what we ask for when we already know the answer but wish we didn't.

The best time to give advice to your children is while they're still young enough to believe you know what you're talking about.

Age

I hope I look as good as my mother does when I reach the age she says she isn't.

The age of some women is like the speedometer on a used car—you know it's set back, but you don't know how far.

* * *

If you want to know how old a woman is, ask her sister-in-law.

—*Edgar Howe*

* * *

You are getting on in years when a dripping faucet starts to cause an uncontrollable bladder urge.

Aging

You are aging if you can remember when it took longer to fly across the country than it did to get to the airport.

* * *

You are aging if you remember when radios plugged into the wall and toothbrushes didn't.

Agnostic

An agnostic is a person who says that he knows nothing about God, and when you agree with him, he becomes angry.

Alarm

An alarm clock is built with a mechanism to scare the daylights into you.

Alcoholic

The trouble with many an alcoholic is that he has no desire to become anonymous.

Algebra

It's strange how few of the world's great problems are solved by people who remember their algebra.

—*Herbert Prochnow*

Allowance

One of the first things a child learns at school is that some other child is getting a bigger allowance.

Alone

Language has created the word *loneliness* to express the pain of being alone, and the word *solitude* to express the glory of being alone.

—*Paul Tillich*

America

America is a land where most citizens vote for Democrats but hope to live like Republicans.

* * *

America is a government of checks and balances: Congress writes the checks, and the people supply the balances.

* * *

The thing that impresses me most about America is the way parents obey their children.

—*Edward VIII*

American

An American is a man who is proud of his right to say what he pleases, and often wishes he had the courage to do so.

Angry

When angry, take a lesson from modern science: Always count down before blasting off.

Answers

He's been that way for years—a born questioner, but he hates answers.

—*Ring Lardner*

Antiques

The frustrating thing about getting old is seeing expensive antiques and remembering items just like them that you threw away.

Appendix

If you still have your appendix at middle age, you are probably a surgeon.

* * *

It's not true that the appendix is useless; it has put thousands of surgeons' wives in fine furs.

April

April is the month when the green returns to the lawn, the trees, and the Internal Revenue Service.

Archives

Archives are where Noah kept his bees.

Argue

Never argue with people who buy ink by the gallon.

—*Tommy Lasorda*

* * *

You may easily play a joke on a man who likes to argue—agree with him.

—*Ed Howe*

Argument

The best way to settle an argument is to step outside before you are invited to.

* * *

The only people who listen to both sides of an argument are the neighbors.

Arrested

Men are not arrested for stealing—they are arrested for being caught at it.

Aspirins

A smart mother suggests that her child bring an apple to his teacher; a smarter mother suggests that he bring a couple aspirins.

Astronauts

If astronauts are so smart, why do they count backward?

Atheist

An atheist cannot find God for the same reason a thief cannot find a policeman.

Athletes

American professional athletes are bilingual: They speak English and profanity.

Author

There are three difficulties in authorship: to write anything worth publishing, to find honest men to publish it, and to get sensible men to read it.

—C. C. Colton

Autobiography

The boss says that he's going to write his autobiography as soon as he can figure out who the main character should be.

Average Out

Things average out: If you think too much of yourself, other people won't.

Babies

Babies are nature's way of telling people what the world looks like at two o'clock in the morning.

Baby

People who say they sleep like a baby usually don't have one.

—Leo J. Burke

Babysitter

It's thrilling when the babysitter calls you at the party and asks where you keep the fire extinguisher.

Bachelor

A bachelor is a man who isn't fit to be tied.

Bachelors

Fools rush in where bachelors fear to wed.

Bad Example

When you get too old to set a bad example, you can always stick around and dish out good advice.

Bad Report

Nowadays, if a kid writes a bad report, he has to bring a note from his computer.

Barber

When one barber cuts another barber's hair, which one does the talking?

* * *

The world is so confusing nowadays; even your barber has trouble giving you all the answers.

Bathtub

I hid my son's Christmas gift where he would never find it—in the bathtub.

Best

Good, better, best; never rest till "good" be "better" and "better," "best."

Best Friend

He took a course on how to be your own best friend and flunked.

Beverly Hills

Last Christmas they went around Beverly Hills giving food packages to people with only one pool.

Big Man

There are two good ways to determine how big a man is: by the size of his friends and by the size of his enemies.

Bill

If it's a bill, the post office will get it to you in 24 hours; if it's a check, allow them a couple of weeks.

—*Richard Needham*

Billboards

Beyond the Alps lies Italy, and beyond the billboards lies America.

Bills

On Father's Day, I can always count on getting one thing: the bills from Mother's Day.

Birth

When I was born I was so surprised I didn't talk for a year and a half.

—*Gracie Allen*

Birthday Cake

By the time she finished lighting the candles on her birthday cake, the first one went out.

* * *

The woman who puts the right number of candles on her birthday cake is playing with fire.

Birthdays

Birthdays are nice, but too many of them will kill a person.

Black and White

When I think of my dad as a little boy, I tend to think of him in black and white.

Blame

He wrecked his car, he lost his job, and yet throughout his life, he took his troubles like a man—he blamed them on his wife.

Blanket

One good turn gets most of the blanket.

Blister

He's like a blister—doesn't show up until all the work is done.

Bluff

The hardest tumble a man can make is to fall over his own bluff.

—*Ambrose Bierce*

Boast

The man who boasts that he always talks the way he thinks should either talk less or think more.

Bolder

When you cannot make up your mind which of two evenly balanced courses of action you should take, choose the bolder.

—*W. J. Slim*

Book

Someday I hope to write a book where the royalties will pay for the copies I give away.

—*Clarence Darrow*

Books

I read part of it all the way through.

—*Sam Goldwyn*

Bore

Bore is too mild a word for some men; they are more like pneumatic drills.

* * *

Some people can stay longer in an hour than others can in a week.

—*W. D. Howells*

* * *

A healthy male adult bore consumes each year one-and-a-half times his own weight in other people's patience.

—*John Updike*

Boss

You can always tell who the boss is: He's the one who watches the clock during the coffee break.

Bottom

Another thing that has to be learned from the bottom up is baby care.

Bowling

If our town didn't have bowling, there would be no culture at all.

Brains

If brains were dynamite, he wouldn't have enough to blow his nose!

Bravery

Bravery is being the only one who knows you're afraid.

—*Franklin P. Jones*

Broad-minded

Many a man who thinks he is broad-minded is merely thickheaded.

Bucket Seats

The trouble with the bucket seats on new cars is that not everybody has the same size bucket.

Buffalo

She's from Buffalo, and you see the resemblance.

Bulletin Board

Sign on a church bulletin board: If you don't like what you hear on a given Sunday, your sins will be cheerfully refunded.

Bullfrog

A cat may have nine lives, but a bullfrog croaks every night.

Bungee Jumping

Whoever invented bungee jumping must have watched a lot of Roadrunner cartoons.

—*Nick Arnette*

Cab Drivers

Cab drivers are living proof that practice does not make perfect.

—*Howard Ogden*

Calamities

Calamities are of two kinds: misfortunes to ourselves, and good fortune to others.

—*Ambrose Bierce*

Candidate

A candidate has to see both sides of an issue; otherwise, how is he going to get around it?

Candy and Flowers

Remember that your wife still enjoys candy and flowers; let her know that you remember by speaking of them occasionally.

Capital Punishment

If you advocate the abolition of capital punishment, remember that you have all the murderers on your side.

Career

Why is it nobody ever asks a man how he combines marriage with a career?

Cats

Cats are smarter than dogs. You can't get eight cats to pull a sled through snow.

—Jeff Valdez

Cemetery

All work and no play makes Jack the wealthiest man in the cemetery.

Censorship

Assassination is the extreme form of censorship.

—George Bernard Shaw

Chameleon

On a slow weekend, put your pet chameleon on a plaid cloth.

Change

Times change: In the old days no one asked how many miles a horse did on a bundle of hay.

* * *

The only time a woman really succeeds in changing a male is when he's a baby.

—*Jacob Braude*

Charge

You are not in charge of the universe: You are in charge of yourself.

—*Arnold Bennett*

Charity

Charity begins at home, and generally dies from lack of outdoor exercise.

Charming

All charming people have something to conceal, usually their total dependence on the appreciation of others.

—*Cyril Connolly*

Check

It may be expensive to reach for the check, but it gets you home earlier.

Cheer

The best way to cheer yourself up is to try to cheer somebody else up.

—*Mark Twain*

Child Guidance

Child guidance is what parents get from their children nowadays.

Child Prodigy

A child prodigy is one with highly imaginative parents.

Children

Never raise your hand to your children—it leaves your midsection unprotected.

—*Robert Orben*

* * *

Cleaning your house while your kids are still growing is like shoveling the walk before it stops snowing.

—*Phyllis Diller*

* * *

If children brighten up a home, it's probably because they never turn off the lights.

* * *

The difference between other people's children and your own is the difference between vice and virtue.

* * *

There are many things you can learn from children—like how much patience you have, for instance.

—*Fran Lebowitz*

* * *

Parents are embarrassed when their children tell lies, and even more embarrassed when they tell the truth.

* * *

Children keep a family together, especially when the parents can't get a babysitter.

* * *

No wonder it's so difficult to raise children properly—they are always imitating their parents.

* * *

Children start kindergarten these days with a big advantage: They already know two letters of the alphabet—*TV.*

Chip

One of the heaviest burdens a person can carry is a chip on his shoulder.

—*Olin Miller*

Christian

Going to church doesn't make you a Christian any more than going to the garage makes you a car.

Church

You have to get to church pretty early to get a seat in the back row.

Circumstantial

Some circumstantial evidence is very strong, as when you find a trout in the milk.

—*Henry David Thoreau*

Class Reunion

Many a man finally gets to a class reunion only to find his classmates so bald and fat that they don't recognize him.

Clean Bill of Health

My doctor says he will give me a clean bill of health as soon as my check clears.

Clever

When a wife laughs at her husband's jokes, it's not because they are clever, but because she is.

Clichés

Avoid clichés like the plague.

Closed Fist

You can't shake hands with a closed fist.

Clothes

The little girl of today starts school with a larger wardrobe than her grandmother had when she got married.

Coffee

The coffee was so weak that I had to help it out of the spout.

* * *

Coffee just isn't my cup of tea.

—*Samuel Goldwyn*

Coffee Breaks

In some government offices there are so many coffee breaks that the employees can't sleep at their work.

Cold Feet

Some people are born with cold feet, some acquire cold feet, and others have cold feet thrust upon them.

College

Another thing that a young man learns at college is that he's terribly short of money.

Comic Strips

There are more comic strips on the beaches than in the newspapers.

Committee

A committee is a group that keeps the minutes and loses hours.

—*Milton Berle*

Committees

Committees have become so important nowadays that subcommittees have to be appointed to do the work.

Communists

If the Communists worked just as hard as they talked, they'd have the most prosperous style of government in the world.

—*Will Rogers*

Compliment

I have been complimented many times and they always embarrass me; I always feel that they have not said enough.

—*Mark Twain*

Conceit

Conceit is God's gift to little men.

—*Bruce Barton*

Conceited

He's so conceited—when he turns away from his mirror, he thinks he's cheating!

Conference

No grand idea was ever born in a conference, but a lot of foolish ideas have died there.

—*F. Scott Fitzgerald*

Confidence

Confidence is that quiet, assured feeling you get just before you fall flat on your face.

Congress

If farmers are paid not to raise crops, why can't we pay Congress not to raise taxes?

* * *

The attitude of Congress toward hidden taxes is not to do away with them, but just to hide them better.

Congressman

No one spends money like a drunken sailor, except a sober congressman.

Conscience

A clear conscience sleeps during thunder.

* * *

My conscience is more trouble and bother to me than anything else I started with.

—*Mark Twain*

* * *

Conscience is the playback of the still, small voice that warned you not to do it in the first place.

Content

He that's content hath enough; he that complains, hath too much.

—*Benjamin Franklin*

Contrary

Some folks are so contrary that if they fell in a river, they'd insist on floating upstream.

—*Josh Billings*

Conventions

Business conventions are important because they demonstrate how many people a company can operate without.

—J. K. Galbraith

Conversation

The art of conversation is not in knowing what you ought to say, but what you ought not to say.

Convinced

A man convinced against his will is of the same opinion still; a woman convinced against her will is a myth.

Counsel

Give neither counsel nor salt till you are asked for it.

Courts

The truth will make you free, unless you're a criminal— then the courts will make you free.

Credit

Next to the man who invented taxes, the one who caused the most trouble in the world is the man who invented credit.

Credit Card

I had my credit card stolen, but I didn't report it because the thief was spending less than my wife did.

—*Henny Youngman*

* * *

If my wife gets one more credit card, she will have a complete deck.

* * *

Money talks, but a credit card uses sign language.

Critic

A critic is a legless man who teaches running.

—*Channing Pollock*

Criticism

If criticism had any real power to harm, the skunk would have been extinct by now.

—*Fred Allen*

Criticizing

The man who is forever criticizing his wife's judgment never seems to question her choice of a husband.

Critics

Taking to pieces is the trade of those who cannot construct.

—*Ralph Waldo Emerson*

Crossword Puzzle

Did you hear about the crossword puzzle addict who died and was buried six feet down and three across?

Cruel Choice

The human race is faced with a cruel choice: work or daytime television.

Curiosity

A bright eye indicates curiosity; a black eye, too much.

Day

Night falls but never breaks, and day breaks but never falls.

Death

Death is nature's way of telling you to slow down.

Debt

Nowadays it's a happy marriage when the couple is as deeply in love as they are in debt.

Deceptive

The difference between us and other people is that their money looks bigger and their troubles smaller.

Decision

A decision is what a man makes when he can't get anyone to serve on a committee.

—*Fletcher Knebel*

Deduction

Few of us ever test our powers of deduction, except when filling out an income tax form.

—*Laurence J. Peter*

Democracy

Democracy is a form of government where you can say what you think, even if you don't think.

* * *

In a democracy you can speak your mind; the only difficulty is to get someone to listen.

Descent

Every beggar is descended from some king, and every king from some beggar.

Despise

A woman nags a man until he does everything she wants him to, and then despises him because he had no mind of his own.

Determination

I am a slow walker, but I never walk backwards.

—*Abraham Lincoln*

Devil

Some people sell themselves to the devil; others rent themselves out by the day.

Diamond

A box of candy means friendship, a bunch of flowers means love, but a diamond means business. The diamond is the hardest stone to get.

Diet

The worst thing about a reducing diet is not watching your food, but watching everyone else's.

* * *

Did you ever notice that in bookstores you will find the diet and exercise books right between humor and fiction?

* * *

A diet is what helps a person gain weight more slowly.

* * *

What's the use of going on a diet where you starve to death just to live longer?

Difficult Secret

The most difficult secret for a man to keep is his own opinion of himself.

—*Marcel Pagnol*

Dinner Party

At a dinner party we should eat wisely but not too well, and talk well but not too wisely.

—*Somerset Maugham*

Diploma

Another way to solve the school dropout problem is to make a high-school diploma a prerequisite for a driver's license.

Diplomat

A diplomat is a man who always remembers a woman's birthday, but never remembers her age.

—*Robert Frost*

* * *

When a diplomat says yes, he means maybe; when he says maybe, he means no; when he says no, he is no diplomat.

Directions

My ancestors wandered in the wilderness for 40 years because even in biblical times, men would not stop to ask for directions.

—*Elayne Boosler*

Dirt

Some women go to the beauty parlor to get a face full of mud and an earful of dirt.

Disadvantages

Many a man works hard and saves money so that his sons won't have the disadvantages that made a man of their father.

Discipline

When a father doesn't have the upper hand with his children, it is usually because he has failed to lower his.

Dishes

Everybody wants to save the earth—nobody wants to help Mom to do the dishes.

—*P. J. O'Rourke*

* * *

You never hear of a man being shot by his wife while doing the dishes.

Disorderly

One of the advantages of being disorderly is that one is constantly making exciting discoveries.

—A. A. Milne

Doctor

The doctor asks the patient what's wrong, and then the patient asks the doctor.

Doctors

Since doctors have stopped making house calls, lots of patients now have to die without their help.

Doesn't Care

The man who doesn't care what other people think is generally found at the top of the ladder or at the bottom.

Dog

Every boy who has a dog should also have a mother so the dog can be fed regularly.

Downcast

A good way to perk up your spirits whenever you are downcast is to think back over the persons you might have married.

Dream House

The trouble with a dream house is that it costs twice as much as you dreamed it would.

Drinking

Many a pedestrian is struck down by a hit-and-rum driver.

Drivers

Drivers are always in a hurry so that they can get in front of you so that they can slow down.

Driving

Drive carefully; don't insist on your rites.

Drops of Water

Little drops of water wear down big stones.

Drum

The first thing a child learns after he gets a drum is that he's never going to get another.

Dumb

I didn't say he was dumb...I said he was 20 years old before he could wave good-bye.

Dying

My grandmother made dying her life's work.

—*Hugh Leonard*

Early American

Nowadays when a woman furnishes her home in Early American style, it probably means she has paid for it in cash.

Earning

Earning money would be a pleasure if it wasn't so taxing.

Eavesdrops

The man who eavesdrops hears himself discussed.

Ecology

Ecology is rather like sex: Each new generation likes to think they were the first to discover it.

—*Michael Allaby*

Economists

If all the nation's economists were laid end to end, they would point in all directions.

Editing

Half the pleasure of recalling the past lies in the editing.

Education

Sixty years ago I knew everything; now I know nothing; education is a progressive discovery of our own ignorance.

—*Will Durant*

* * *

America believes in education: The average professor earns more money in a year than the professional athlete earns in a whole week.

—*Evan Esar*

Effort

Everything requires effort—the only thing you can achieve without it is failure.

Egotist

Give the egotist his due—he never goes around talking about other people.

* * *

An egotist may be all I's, yet he cannot see anything but himself.

Eighty

Life can be pretty grim when you pass 80, especially if there's a state trooper behind you.

Einstein's Brain

My boss has a brain like Einstein's—dead since 1955.

—*Gene Perret*

Ends

Why is it every time you start to make ends meet, somebody comes along and moves the ends?

Enemy

It takes your enemy and your friend, working together, to hurt you to the heart; the one to slander you, and the other to get the news to you.

—*Mark Twain*

Engagement

The proof that women can keep secrets is that a woman may be engaged for months before telling her fiancé about it.

English

Why talk baby talk to an infant when plain English is hard enough for the poor youngster to understand?

—*John Kendrick Bangs*

Enjoy

If you don't enjoy your own company, you're probably right.

Enthusiasm

Nothing dispels enthusiasm like a small admission fee.

—*Kin Hubbard*

Error

A man can build a staunch reputation for honesty by admitting he was in error, especially when he gets caught at it.

—*Robert Ruark*

Etiquette

Etiquette is knowing how to yawn with your mouth closed.

Everything

The woman who has everything should be given a course in sales resistance.

Evolution

If evolution really worked, nature would have long ago produced pedestrians with wings.

Exasperating

There is nothing so exasperating as arguing with someone who knows what he's talking about.

Excuses

When it comes to excuses, the world is full of great inventors.

Executive

An executive is a man who is always annoying the hired help by asking them to do something.

Exercise

Some people exercise by jumping to conclusions, some by sidestepping their responsibilities, but most people get it by running down their friends.

* * *

The only exercise some people get is when their electric toothbrushes break down.

* * *

Anybody who says he runs 20 miles a day with his muscles stretching, his legs pounding, his heart beating like a drum, and his lungs on fire because it makes him feel great will lie about everything else, too.

* * *

My wife's idea of exercise is to shop faster.

Exit

Three-quarters of our population live in or near cities; the other quarter is on the highway looking for the exit.

Experience

There's only one thing more painful than learning from experience, and that is not learning from experience.

* * *

At 20 you blush when a man praises you; at 30 you think him clever; at 40 you wonder what he wants.

* * *

Experience is a teacher who never tells you in advance what your next lesson is to be.

Extension Cord

Did you hear about the teenager who plans to run away from home just as soon as she gets a long enough extension cord?

Extremes

Formerly the younger generation often went to extremes, but nowadays they often start from there.

Fail

Since three out of four small businesses fail, my recommendation is to start a large business.

Failure

The man who always criticizes others for his failures never credits others for his successes.

* * *

Success comes in cans, failure in can'ts.

* * *

It is hard to admire a man who makes a success out of what you gave up as a failure.

Faith

A man achieves according to what he believes.

Fame

The fame of great men ought to be judged always by the means they used to acquire it.

—*La Rochefoucauld*

Family

All happy families resemble one another, but each unhappy family is unhappy in its own way.

Family Tree

Don't pay money to have your family tree traced; just go into politics and your opponents will do it for you.

Farm

A farm is a parcel of land on which, if you get up early enough in the morning and work late at night, you'll make a fortune—if you strike oil.

Fat

In food, fat settles at the top; in folk, fat settles on the bottom.

Fat Chance

How come "fat chance" and "slim chance" mean the same thing?

Father

A boy's best friend is his father, and if he gets up early or stays up late he may get to see him.

Father's Day

Mother's Day and Father's Day are alike, except that on Father's Day you buy a cheaper gift.

Faults

Women's faults are many,
Men have only two:
Everything they say
And everything they do.

* * *

The faults of other people are like headlights of an approaching car—they always seem more glaring than our own.

* * *

Don't criticize your husband's faults; if it weren't for them, he might have married a better wife.

Favor

To accept a favor from a friend is to confer one.

—*John Churton Collins*

Fear

The man who doesn't know the meaning of the word *fear* probably doesn't know many other words either.

Ferocity

Ferocity is still characteristic of bulls and other vegetarians.

—*George Bernard Shaw*

Few Words

He's a man of few words, but he keeps repeating them.

Fight

It isn't the size of the dog in the fight that counts; it's the size of the fight in the dog.

Fish

I caught a fish so big that the Polaroid weighed nine pounds.

* * *

You can't tell: Maybe a fish goes home and lies about the size of the man he got away from.

Five More Pounds

If I put on five more pounds I will be eligible for state-hood.

—*Audrey Buslik*

Flashlight

A flashlight is a great gadget for storing dead batteries.

Flattery

The best way to get someone to listen to reason is to mix some flattery with it.

Flood

There's only one thing worse than a flooded basement, and that's a flooded attic.

Fly

A fly, sir, may sting a stately horse and make him wince; but one is but an insect, and the other is a horse still.

—*Samuel Johnson*

Fog

If a tin whistle is made of tin, what is a foghorn made of?

Folksingers

There are two kinds of folksingers: those who can sing and won't, and those who can't sing and do.

Food

Children are always being told to eat more by parents who are always being told to eat less.

Fool

Before a man speaks, it is always safe to assume that he is a fool; after he speaks, it is seldom necessary to assume.

—*H. L. Mencken*

*   *   *

It is better to keep your mouth shut and be thought a fool than to open it and remove all doubt.

*   *   *

A fool empties his head every time he opens his mouth.

*   *   *

If all the cars in the country were placed end to end, some fool would still pull out and try to pass them.

*   *   *

You can always tell a fool, unless he's hiding inside you.

*   *   *

A fool and his money are soon parted, but seldom by another fool.

*   *   *

You can only fool some of the people some of the time because the rest of the time they are trying to fool you.

Foolish

God made woman beautiful and foolish: beautiful, that man might love her, and foolish, that she might love him.

Foot

Every time he opens his mouth, his foot falls out.

Footprints

Some men may not leave footprints on the sands of time, but they certainly leave them everywhere else.

Foreign Aid

America's foreign-aid policy is an open book—an open checkbook.

Forgetfulness

Forgetfulness is a virtue only when you can remember the right things to forget.

Forgiveness

Forgiveness is the fragrance the violet dashes on the heel that crushes it.

—*Mark Twain*

Forty

I am just turning 40 and taking my time about it.

Forty-eight

I'm 60, but if there were 15 months in every year, I'd only be 48.

—*James Thurber*

Four Types of People

Society is built on four types of people: performers, conformers, reformers, and miss-informers.

Fox

You don't set a fox to watching the chickens just because he has a lot of experience in the hen house.

—*Harry S. Truman*

Friend

A true friend laughs at your stories even when they're not so good, and sympathizes with your troubles even when they're not so bad.

* * *

You can always tell a real friend: When you've made a fool of yourself, he doesn't feel you've done a permanent job.

Friends

Be kind to your friends; without them, you would be a stranger.

Frontiersman

A frontiersman nowadays is one who moves into a house at the edge of a new subdivision.

Funeral

I did not attend his funeral, but I wrote a nice letter saying I approved it.

—*Mark Twain*

Funerals

If you don't go to people's funerals, they won't come to yours.

Futility of Riches

The Scriptures first taught the futility of riches, but it took an income tax to drive the lesson home.

Future

I never think of the future. It comes soon enough.

—*Albert Einstein*

Garbage

In California they don't throw their garbage away—they turn it into TV shows.

Garden

A garden is a thing of beauty and a job forever.

Gardener

Nothing discourages an amateur gardener like watching his family eat the entire garden at one meal.

Gas

The only motorist who never seems to run out of gas is the backseat driver.

Genius

Genius learns from nature, talent from books.

—*Josh Billings*

Gentleman

A gentleman is a man who can play the trumpet but doesn't.

—*Lord Chesterfield*

Gift

It would help if we had the gift of seeing other people as they see themselves.

Girl Scout

In my rich neighborhood, the girls go around selling Girl Scout croissants.

Giving

A good way to judge a man is by what he says, a better way is by what he does, and the best way is by what he gives.

Glass Houses

People who live in glass houses make the most interesting neighbors.

Glutton

Sleep is the only thing that keeps a glutton from eating 24 hours a day.

Going Away Party

When I went to college, my parents threw a going away party for me, according to the letter.

—*Emo Philips*

Golf

About the time a man gets his temper under control, he goes out and plays golf again.

* * *

A lot of ministers don't play golf because they don't have the vocabulary for it.

Good

Good often comes from evil: The apple that Eve ate has given work to thousands of designers and dressmakers.

Good Breeding

Good breeding consists of concealing how much we think of ourselves and how little we think of the other person.

—*Mark Twain*

Good Communication

Good communication is as stimulating as black coffee, and just as hard to sleep after.

—*Anne Morrow Lindbergh*

Good Memory

Writing things down is the best secret of a good memory.

Good Sport

The only drawback in being a good sport is that you have to lose to prove it.

Good Thing

Lots of people know a good thing the minute the other fellow sees it first.

Gossip

Conversation between Adam and Eve must have been difficult at times because they had nobody to talk about.

—*Agnes Repplier*

For gossip to succeed, it has to be unreasonable enough to shock everyone and reasonable enough that a few will believe it.

*   *   *

Most of the fiction in this world comes from people who are repeating true stories.

*   *   *

The light a gossip throws on her neighbors is always a reflection.

*   *   *

A gossip's idea of generosity is to keep nothing to herself.

Government

The nearest approach to immorality on earth is a government bureau.

—*James F. Byrnes*

Grandchildren

Grandchildren don't make a man feel old; it's the knowledge that he's married to a grandmother.

—*G. Norman Collie*

Gravity

It's a good thing there's gravity or else when birds died, they'd stay where they were.

—*Steven Wright*

Greed

Nothing is enough for the man to whom enough is too little.

—*Epicurus*

Grief

It is foolish to tear one's hair in grief, as if grief could be lessened by baldness.

—*Cicero*

Guests

There are two kinds of guests: those who come before dinner, and those who come after dinner.

Habit

Habit is habit, and not to be flung out of the window by any man, but coaxed downstairs a step at a time.

—*Mark Twain*

Habits

The second half of a man's life is made up of nothing but the habits he has acquired during the first half.

—*Dostoyevsky*

Habit-Forming

Most tranquilizers are not habit-forming, at least not if you take them every day.

Half-Truth

It is twice as hard to crush a half-truth as a whole lie.

—*Austin O'Malley*

Happiness

Happiness is good health and a bad memory.

Happy

It's better to be happy than wise.

* * *

Most folks are about as happy as they make up their minds to be.

—*Abraham Lincoln*

Happy Marriage

A happy marriage is one where the man knows what to remember, and the woman knows what to forget.

Hard of Hearing

Blessed are the hard of hearing, for they shall miss much idle gossip.

Hard Work

When a man tells you he got rich through hard work, ask him, "Whose?"

—*Don Marquis*

Harp

Imagine a guy who plays the harp all of his life, and when he dies, he doesn't go to heaven.

Hate

The man has no occasion to hate me—I can't recall that I ever did him a favor.

—*Disraeli*

Health

Nothing gives his friends more pleasure than when a health faddist becomes ill.

Healthy People

Healthy people have one thing in common: They always give advice to the sick.

Heaven

There will be lots of people in heaven just as surprised to see you there as you will be to see them.

Hell

Where do the people in hell tell each other to go?

Hero

A hero is no braver than an ordinary man, but he is braver five minutes longer.

—*Ralph Waldo Emerson*

High Point

The other night, while lying on a couch, I reviewed the high point of my life and fell asleep!

History

History is simply a piece of paper covered with print; the main thing is still to make history, not to write it.

—*Bismarck*

Hollywood

Strip away the phony tinsel of Hollywood and you find the real tinsel underneath.

—*Oscar Levant*

Home

What's the good of a home if you are never in it?

—*George Grossmith and Weedon Grossmith*

Home Improvement

I went to the bank for a home improvement loan, and they gave me $2000 to move out of the neighborhood.

Honesty

He that loses his honesty has nothing else to lose.

Honor

The louder he talked of his honor, the faster we counted our spoons.

—*Ralph Waldo Emerson*

Horseback Ride

There's nothing like your first horseback ride to make you feel better off.

Horse Thief

The man who steals another man's wife is no better than a horse thief.

Human

To err is human; to blame it on someone else is even more human.

Human Nature

The trouble with human nature is that there are too many people connected to it.

Humdinger

I once crossed a bee with a doorbell, and I got a humdinger.

Humor

Humor is, by its nature, more truthful than factual.

—P. J. O'Rourke

Hustle

All things come to him who hustles while he waits.

Hypochondriac

A hypochondriac never gets cured of any disease until he acquires another.

I Do

There are no words in the English language that lead to as many quarrels as "I do."

Idea

Nothing is more dangerous than an idea, when a man has only one idea.

—Alain

Ignorance

If ignorance is bliss, why aren't there more happy teenagers?

* * *

You can't underestimate the ignorance of some people.

*   *   *

If ignorance paid dividends, everyone would make a fortune in the stock market.

Illegitimate

I refuse to admit I'm more than 52, even if that does make my sons illegitimate.

—*Lady Astor*

Imitate

When people are free to do as they please, they usually imitate each other.

—*Eric Hoffer*

Immature

You are only young once, but you can always be immature.

—*Dave Barry*

Impolite

It is impolite for a man to fall asleep while his wife is talking, but a man has to sleep sometime.

Impress

Many of us live expensively to impress our friends who live expensively to impress us.

In a Minute

Take off your clothes; the doctor will be with you in a minute.

Income Tax

The income tax is a neat plan devised to clean you out of your filthy lucre.

* * *

Today it takes more brains and effort to make out the income tax form than it does to make the income.

—*Alfred E. Neuman*

Indecisive

I used to be indecisive, but now I'm not so sure.

Index

A friend of mine is compiling an index for the dictionary.

Infatuation

Infatuation is a disease usually cured by marriage.

Inferiority

The trouble with an inferiority complex is that the people who ought to have it, never do.

Inflation

Inflation marches on, making it possible for people in all walks of life to live in more expensive neighborhoods without ever moving.

Insane

Some men are born insane, some achieve insanity, and some go in for psychoanalysis.

Insight

Hindsight is good, foresight is better, but insight is the best of all.

Insomnia

What you don't worry about gives someone else insomnia.

Inspiration

Work sometimes comes from inspiration, but more often inspiration comes from work.

Insults

There are two insults no human being will endure: that he has no sense of humor, and that he has never known trouble.

—*Sinclair Lewis*

Insurance

Why is it that insurance people always talk about death benefits?

Intolerance

If there's one thing I can't stand, its intolerance.

Introduction

After such an introduction, I can hardly wait to hear what I'm going to say.

—Evelyn Anderson

Invisible Ink

How do you tell when you've run out of invisible ink?

Irritating

Nothing is more irritating than not being invited to a party you wouldn't be caught dead at.

—Bill Vaughan

Jack and Jill

All work and no play makes Jack a dull boy—and Jill a wealthy widow.

—Evan Esar

Job

It's a recession when your neighbor loses his job; it's a depression when you lose yours.

—Harry S. Truman

Jogging

Since jogging came along, more people are collapsing in perfect health.

Journey

A journey of a thousand miles begins with a delay of about three hours.

Judge

A judge is a man who ends a sentence with a sentence.

Judgment

Everyone complains of his memory, no one of his judgment.

—*La Rochefoucauld*

Karate

He was a karate expert, but one day he joined the army, saluted, and killed himself.

Kick

If you could kick the person responsible for most of your troubles, you wouldn't be able to sit down for months.

Kiss

A kiss is not enough for one, just enough for two, and too much for three.

Kleptomaniac

Then there was a patient who told the doctor he was a kleptomaniac and wondered if there was something he could take for it.

Knocked Out

I was knocked out so often, they sold advertising space on the soles of my shoes.

Knowledge

The less you know about a subject, the longer it takes you to explain it.

Laugh

If you're not allowed to laugh in heaven, I don't want to go there.

—Martin Luther

Lawyer

I do not wish to speak ill of any man behind his back, but I believe that gentleman is a lawyer.

—Samuel Johnson

* * *

A lawyer is a learned gentleman who rescues your estate from your enemies and keeps it for himself.

—David Lodge

* * *

How can a lawyer write a document of 5,000 words and call it a "brief"?

Lawyers

If crime doesn't pay, how come so many people want to be lawyers?

* * *

When asked to contribute ten dollars to a lawyer's funeral, I said: "Here's fifty. Bury five of them."

—*Melvin Helitzer*

Lazy

More people would get to the top if someone discovered a way to sit down and slide uphill.

Leadership

No one leads the orchestra without turning his back on the crowd.

Leave Home

The reason more wives than husbands leave home is that few men know how to pack their own suitcases.

Legacies

If people would leave their legacies to their lawyers, it would save a lot of time.

Lend

Never lend your car to anyone you gave birth to.

Letter

If you leave a letter unopened long enough, it answers itself.

Liar

A person who is a good liar got that way by long practice.

—*Herbert V. Prochnow*

Liberty

Eternal vigilance is the price of liberty.

Lie

A lie can travel halfway round the world while truth is putting its pants on.

Life

The first 40 years of life give us the text, the next 30 the commentary.

—*Schopenhauer*

Life Expectancy

Life expectancy is steadily increasing, probably to enable us to complete the time payments.

Lightning

Lightning never strikes twice in the same place because, after its hit, the same place isn't there anymore.

* * *

Thunder is impressive, but it is lightning that does the work.

—*Mark Twain*

Listener

A good listener is not only popular everywhere, but after a while he knows something.

Litigant

Litigant: a person about to give up his skin for the hope of retaining his bone.

—*Ambrose Bierce*

Loans

The man who writes the bank's advertising slogan is not the same man who makes the loans.

—*George Coote*

Logic

Logic is like the sword: Those who appeal to it shall perish by it.

—*Samuel Butler*

Long Life

The only group of people who seem to have discovered the secret of long life are rich relatives.

Looking Back

If you look back too much, you will soon be heading that way.

Losing Face

Another way in which a woman loses face is by misplacing her cosmetic kit.

Lost in Thought

When a man is lost in thought, it's probably because he's in unfamiliar territory.

Lots to Do

There is no fun in having nothing to do; the fun is in having lots to do and not doing it.

Lottery

I figure you have the same chance of winning the lottery whether you play or not.

—*Fran Lebowitz*

Love

Love is the only fire against which there is no insurance.

* * *

Love is like an hourglass, with the heart filling up as the brain empties.

—*Jules Renard*

* * *

Love may be blind, but it certainly finds its way around in the dark.

Lover

All the world loves a lover, but laughs when it gets hold of his love letters.

Luck

I believe in luck: How else can you explain the success of those you dislike?

—*Jean Cocteau*

* * *

What luck for rulers that men do not think.

—*Adolf Hitler*

Lying

There's a curious sort of statute of limitations in the learned world which makes it impossible to call a man a liar if he has gone on lying successfully for 50 years.

—*Ronald A. Knox*

Mailing List

Some people have their names perpetuated in stone or cast in bronze, but most of us are on mailing lists.

Making Things Happen

Some people make things happen, some watch things happen, while others wonder what has happened.

Manuscript

I wasn't overly sensitive when the publisher returned my manuscript, but I was hurt when he sent it by junk mail.

Marriage

Marriage is the most expensive way of discovering your faults.

* * *

Marriage is an institution where he rules the roost, and she rules the rooster.

* * *

If love is a dream, then marriage is an alarm clock.

* * *

The man who marries in order to have someone to tell his troubles to, soon has plenty to talk about.

* * *

Love is blind, and marriage is an eye-opener.

* * *

If it weren't for marriage, husbands and wives would have to quarrel with strangers.

Married

A man may be a fool and not know it, but not if he is married.

—*H. L. Mencken*

* * *

You can't always tell a married man just by looking at him: He may be a bachelor with a headache.

Married Life

Married life teaches many lessons: One of them is to think of things far enough in advance not to say them.

Mars

I am absolutely sure there is no life on Mars—it's not listed on my teenage daughter's phone bills.

—*Larry Mathews*

Mature

The reason mature men look younger than mature women is that a woman of 40 is usually 50.

Mealtime

Mealtime is when the youngsters continue eating but sit down.

Memory

There are three kinds of memory: good, bad, and convenient.

Men

The American male doesn't mature until he has exhausted all other possibilities.

—*Wilfrid Sheed*

Men's Suits

The reason men's suits look the same year after year is that most men are wearing the same ones.

Mercy

Children are innocent and love justice, while most adults are wicked and prefer mercy.

—*G. K. Chesterton*

Middle Age

Middle age is the period when a woman's hair starts turning from gray to black.

* * *

Middle age is when, wherever you go on holiday, you pack a sweater.

* * *

Middle age is when you have met so many people that every new person you meet reminds you of someone else and usually is.

—*Ogden Nash*

* * *

One of the chief pleasures of middle age is looking back at the people you didn't marry.

* * *

The worst thing about middle age is that you outgrow it.

* * *

Middle age is the time in life when you are determined to cut down on your calories one of these days.

Middle of the Road

Standing in the middle of the road is very dangerous; you get knocked down by the traffic from both sides.

—*Margaret Thatcher*

Milk and Honey

The land of milk and honey has its drawbacks: You can get kicked by a cow and stung by a bee.

Mind

Her mind is always on the tip of her tongue.

Minister

The only way a minister can meet his flock is to join a golf club.

Miserable

I feel so miserable without you, it's almost like having you here.

—*Stephen Bishop*

Misery

Misery is putting something in a safe place and never being able to find it.

* * *

Misery loves company, but can't bear competition.

—*Josh Billings*

Misspelled

If a word in the dictionary is misspelled, how would we know?

Mistake

It is foolish to make the same mistake when there are so many varieties to choose from.

Mistakes

Learn from the mistakes of others—you can't live long enough to make them all yourself.

—*Martin Vanbee*

Modern Apartments

The trouble with modern apartments is that the walls are too thin when you try to sleep, and too thick when you try to listen.

Modern Art

Understanding modern art is like trying to figure out the plot in a bowl of alphabet soup.

Modesty

Modesty is the feeling that other people will discover how great you are.

Money

Money may not buy happiness, but with it you can be unhappy in comfort.

* * *

Money can't buy happiness, but it helps you to look for it in many more places.

* * *

Money may not buy you more friends, but it does attract a better class of enemies.

* * *

Money has wings, and most of us see only the tail feathers.

* * *

Another reason you cannot take money with you is that it goes before you do.

Mop

Don't tell a teenager that her hair looks like a mop; she probably doesn't know what a mop is.

Mother

No matter how old a mother is, she still watches her middle-aged children for signs of improvement.

—*Florida Scott-Maxwell*

Mother's Day

Give your mother something she can be grateful for on Mother's Day: Move out!

Mountain Climbers

Mountain climbers always rope themselves together, probably to prevent the sensible ones from going home.

Mud

Mud thrown is ground lost.

Naïve

Oh, what a tangled web do parents weave when they think that their children are naïve.

—*Ogden Nash*

Name-Dropping

There's nothing girls enjoy more than dropping names, especially their maiden names.

National Bird

Our national bird is the eagle, with the stork a close second.

Natural Childbirth

My wife did natural childbirth—no eye makeup, no lipstick, no rouge...

Neglected

If you feel neglected by your family, think of Whistler's father.

Neighbors

It's really unbelievable how many mistakes the neighbors can make in raising their children.

New Idea

Every time a man puts a new idea across, he finds ten men who thought of it before he did—but they only thought of it.

New Year's Resolutions

Most New Year's resolutions go in one year and out the other.

New York

Anybody in New York who speaks good English must be a foreigner.

No Work

No bees, no honey; no work, no money.

Nobody Cares

If you think nobody cares about you, try missing a couple of mortgage payments.

Noise

What a terrible din there would be if we all made as much noise when things go right as we do when things go wrong!

Nothing

The way to be nothing is to do nothing.

—*Ed Howe*

Nothing to Say

There's nothing wrong with having nothing to say; the trick is not to say it aloud.

Obscene

What is this world coming to? I hear they just arrested a fellow who talks dirty to plants. They caught him making an obscene fern call!

Obstacles

If it weren't for obstacles, we would never know whether we really want something or merely think we do.

Office Clock

An office clock is rarely stolen—probably because everyone watches it.

Officials

The trouble with officials is they just don't care who wins.

—*Tommy Canterbury*

Old

The worst thing about growing old is having to listen to a lot of advice from one's children.

* * *

I won't say he's old, but his car insurance covers fire, theft, and Indian raids.

Old Age

Another objection to old age is that there's not much of a future in it.

Old Popular Songs

The old popular songs are best, especially those that are not sung any longer.

Older

I used to dread getting older because I thought I would not be able to do all the things I wanted to do, but now that I am older I find that I don't want to do them.

—*Lady Nancy Astor*

* * *

You know you are getting older when "happy hour" is a nap.

—*Gray Kristofferson*

Old-Timer

An old-timer is one who remembers when a juvenile delinquent was a youngster returning from the wood-shed.

Open Mind

Keep an open mind, but don't keep it too open or people will throw a lot of rubbish into it.

Opera

When an opera star sings her head off, she usually improves her appearance.

—*Victor Borge*

Opportunity

When opportunity knocks, some people wait for it to break the door down and come in.

* * *

If opportunity ever knocks on our kids' door, it better come during a commercial break.

Opposite Sex

They are called the opposite sex because, when you think you have fooled them, it is just the opposite.

Optimist

If it wasn't for the optimist, the pessimist wouldn't know how happy he isn't.

Outgo

When your outgo exceeds your income, your upkeep is your downfall.

Pack Rat

Why is it that you keep something for many years, and then give it away only a few weeks before you need it?

Pair

It wasn't an apple from the tree that started the trouble in the Garden of Eden; it was the pair on the ground.

Parachute

If your parachute doesn't open up for you, you've obviously jumped to a conclusion.

Parents

We get our parents when they are too old for us to change their habits.

Party

Never give a party if you will be the most interesting person there.

—Mickey Friedman

Pat

Every child should have an occasional pat on the back as long as it is applied low enough and hard enough.

—Fulton J. Sheen

Patience

It's important that mothers with small children save something for a rainy day—patience.

* * *

Patience is the ability to stand something as long as it happens to the other fellow.

Pause

He talks at the drop of a pause.

—*John Mason Brown*

Peace and Quiet

For people who like peace and quiet, get a phoneless cord.

Pedestrian

A pedestrian is a person walking or lying in the street.

Personality

He has the personality of a dial tone!

Pessimist

A pessimist remembers that the lily belongs to the onion family; an optimist, that the onion belongs to the lily family.

Pest

The first day, a guest; the second, a burden; the third, a pest.

—*Edouard R. Laboulaye*

Phone Calls

Half the phone calls would never be answered if we knew in advance who was calling.

Pi

What do you get if you divide the circumference of a pumpkin by its diameter? Pumpkin pi.

Pilgrim

He's been in so many turkeys; he should be made an honorary Pilgrim.

Poem

My favorite poem is the one that starts "Thirty days hath September" because it actually tells you something.

Poets

Poets all have imagination because they imagine people are going to read their poems.

Policeman

I wanted to be a policeman, but discovered I was allergic to doughnuts.

Polite

If any of you are related to our main guest, let me know so I can speak slowly.

—*Wendy Morgan*

Politician

A politician has a good chance of going to heaven—they say that hot air rises.

* * *

Many a candidate feels that since his rival has been fooling the public for years, he should now be given a chance.

Politicians

Old politicians never die—they just run once too often.

Pollution

There's so much pollution in the air now that if it weren't for our lungs there'd be no place to put it.

—*Robert Orben*

Poor

The advantage of being poor is that a doctor will cure you faster.

Pop

Times have changed: In the ol' days, before you could pop the question, you had to question her pop.

Popular

He was the toast of two continents—Greenland and Australia.

—Dorothy Parker

Poverty

Poverty is a wonderful thing: It sticks to a man even when all his friends forsake him.

Practice

Everybody ought to do at least two things each day that he hates to do, just for practice.

—William James

* * *

If practice makes perfect and nobody's perfect, then why practice?

Praise

He who praises everybody, praises nobody.

—Samuel Johnson

Prejudice

Another labor-saving device is prejudice: It enables you to form opinions without having to dig up the facts.

Preparation

If you will spend more time sharpening the ax, you will spend less time chopping wood.

Prices

The most beautiful sound is never heard—the sound of falling prices.

Pride

When someone sings his own praises, he always gets the tune too high.

—*Mary Waldrip*

Principal

What most youngsters object to about school is the principal of the thing.

Probably

A pinch of probably is worth a pound of perhaps.

—*James Thurber*

Procrastination

Procrastination is a habit most people put off trying to correct.

Professors

Old professors never die; they merely lose their faculties.

Progress

Progress means taking risks, for you can't steal home and keep your foot on third.

Prosperity

Prosperity is a fleeting interval between the last installment and the next down payment.

Psychiatrist

When a psychiatrist treats a person with a split personality, does he charge him double?

* * *

A psychiatrist is a person who will listen to you as long as you don't make sense.

* * *

Anybody who goes to see a psychiatrist ought to have his head examined.

Psychiatry

Psychiatry is the science that has turned the old-fashioned sins of yesterday into the emotional ills of today.

Psychoanalyst

A psychoanalyst is a person who reads between the lines, even when there is nothing there.

Psychological

All analysts are psychological, but some are more psycho than logical.

Public Speakers

Too many public speakers begin by saying they have nothing to say, and then take an hour to prove it.

—*William Lyon Phelps*

*   *   *

Some public speakers are applauded when they stand up, but most are applauded when they sit down.

Punctuality

Punctuality is a virtue, but only if it is combined with patience.

Quarrel

It takes two to make a quarrel, and the same number to get married.

Quarterbacks

Old quarterbacks never die; they just fade back and pass away.

Questions

Judge a man by his questions rather than his answers.

—*Voltaire*

Racehorse

A racehorse is the only creature that can take thousands of people for a ride at the same time.

Radio

The other day somebody broke into my brother's car and put in a better radio.

Railroad Crossing

The man who hasn't time to stop at a railroad crossing always finds time to attend the funeral.

Rake

The rake's progress is slowest when there's a boy at the end of the handle.

Reading

Reading the book before seeing the movie always makes it more difficult to guess the plot.

Recessions

Economic recessions wouldn't be so bad if they didn't come when so many people were out of work.

Red to Green

The faster way to get the light to turn from red to green is to look for something in the glove compartment.

Referee

Having one child makes you a parent; having two makes you a referee.

Refrigerator

A refrigerator is a place where you store leftovers until they are ready to be thrown out.

Relative

Everything is relative: You're expendable when you ask for a raise, but indispensable when you ask for a day off.

Relax

He likes to relax over a cup of coffee, sometimes for three or four months.

Remember

It isn't so astonishing, the number of things I can remember, as the number of things I can remember that aren't so.

—*Mark Twain*

Report Card

The first time many of us realize that a little learning is a dangerous thing is when we bring home a poor report card.

Reputation

Your character is built by what you stand for, your reputation by what you fall for.

Resignations

It seems that nothing ever gets to going good till there's a few resignations.

—*Kin Hubbard*

Respect

There was no respect for youth when I was young, and now I am old, there is no respect for age—I missed it coming and going.

—*J. B. Priestley*

Resting

Nothing reminds a woman of all the things her husband has to do around the house like the sight of him resting.

Resumés

Life is what you make it, which could explain a lot of resumés.

Retire

Before you decide to retire, stay home and watch some of the daytime television programs.

Retired

The other day he retired from his job, and nobody knew.

Retirement

When a man retires and time is no longer a matter of urgent importance, his colleagues generally present him with a watch.

—*R. C. Sherriff*

Rich

Every morning I get up and look through the Forbes list of the richest people in America. If I'm not there, I go to work.

—*Robert Orben*

Right Track

It isn't enough to be on the right track; you are liable to get run over if you just stay there.

Risk

And the trouble is, if you don't risk anything, you risk even more.

—*Erica Jong*

Rob

Some men rob Peter to pay Paul, while others rob Peter to pay Pauline.

Rod

Don't spare the rod, or you may someday find Junior carrying one.

Roost

The future is the past come home to roost.

Royally

I told my girl I was taking her out royally, so we ate at the Burger King and the Dairy Queen.

Rumors

I hate to spread rumors, but what else can one do with them?

—*Amanda Lear*

Salary

The most serious impediment to marriage nowadays is the difficulty of supporting both a family and the government on one salary.

Santa

There are a lot of names for Santa: There's Kris Kringle, Saint Nicholas, MasterCard, Visa, and Discover.

Saving

Saving is a very fine thing, especially when your parents have done it for you.

Scare

A good scare is usually worth more to a person than good advice.

School Bus Driver

Everyone is in awe of the lion tamer in a cage with half a dozen lions—everyone but a school-bus driver.

Science

The ways of science are unpredictable: It can get men up to the moon, but it cannot get pigeons down from public buildings.

Scientists

Scientists are trying to find intelligent beings on other planets, probably because they have given up the search here on earth.

Sculptor

You show me a sculptor who works in the basement, and I'll show you a low-down chiseler!

—Soupy Sales

Second Look

The cure for love at first sight is to take a second look.

Secret

Some people's idea of keeping a secret is to refuse to tell who told it to them.

Seldom What They Seem

Things are seldom what they seem—that's why people mistake education for intelligence, wealth for happiness, and sex for love.

Self-Control

Golf develops a beginner's self-control, but caddying for a beginner develops it even more.

Self-Preservation

Self-preservation is the first law of nature, with lying a close second.

Sense of Humor

You can test a person's sense of humor by what he laughs at and his sense of values by what he doesn't laugh at.

Shallow

Deep down I'm really shallow.

—*Linda Merkin*

Share

When there's food for eight, there's enough for ten.

—*Moliére*

Shopping

The most a man can hope for when he goes shopping with his wife is that her feet will start to hurt before his wallet does.

Shoveling Snow

Shoveling the snow off your walk may be hard work, but it's easier than to get your teenage son to do it.

Shrink

You can go to a shrink slightly cracked, and before you get done, you're broke.

Silence

Silence isn't always golden; sometimes it is just plain yellow.

* * *

Silence is not always tact, and it is tact that is golden, not silence.
—*Samuel Butler*

* * *

Another advantage that silence has is that it cannot be repeated.

* * *

My wife suffers in silence louder than anyone I know.

Silent Contempt

Silent contempt is the noblest way a man can express himself when the other fellow is bigger.

Simple

Most girls are attracted to the simple things in life, like men.

Simple Life

There's nothing more complicated today than trying to lead a simple life.

Sin

One of the reasons why sin is so attractive is because it is so well advertised.

Sing

If you must sing while bathing, do it under a shower, not in the tub; the sound of running water is a great help.

Singing

The first Sunday I sang in the church choir, 200 people changed their religion.

—*Fred Allen*

Sit Down

Please sit down before someone less desirable sits next to me.

Six Months

My doctor gave me six months to live, but when I couldn't pay the bill, he gave me six months more.

—*Walter Matthau*

Skiing

I have a special way of falling down—it's called skiing.

Ski Jump

A ski jump is a leap made by a person on his way to the hospital.

Skunk

A skunk in the bush is worth two in the hand.

Slacks

If the hindsight of some women were as good as their foresight, they wouldn't be wearing slacks.

Sleep

The amount of sleep required by the average person is about half an hour more.

Sleepwalking

The only virtue in sleepwalking is that you get your exercise and your rest at the same time.

Slum

I wasn't born in a slum, but my family moved into one as soon as we could afford it.

—*Melville Landon*

Small Town

If nobody knows the troubles you've seen, you are probably not living in a small town.

Smile

Show me a man who smiles when everything goes wrong, and I'll show you an idiot.

* * *

Let a smile be your umbrella, and you'll get a mouthful of rain.

Smoking

No one gives up smoking without substituting something for it, like boasting.

* * *

It's better for a person to be smoking here on earth than in the hereafter.

Snore

He snored so loud that we thought he was driving his hogs to market.

—Jonathan Swift

* * *

Another mystery that has never been solved is why people who snore are always the ones who fall asleep first.

Solitude

Solitude is a good place to visit but a poor place to stay.

—Josh Billings

Sorry

Don't feel sorry for yourself; feel sorry for those who have to live with you.

Space

Some students take up the arts in college, some take up the sciences, while others just take up space.

Spade

Many a man calls a spade a spade until he accidentally trips over one.

Speak

The ability to speak several languages is an asset, but the ability to keep your mouth shut in one language is priceless.

Specialist

A specialist is a person who knows very much about very little and continues to learn more and more about less and less until eventually he knows practically everything about almost nothing at all.

Speech

It should take two weeks to prepare a half-hour speech, one week to prepare an hour speech, but no time at all to prepare a two-hour speech.

* * *

Why shouldn't speech be free since very little of it is worth anything?

Speeding

The way many a motorist speeds through traffic, you would think he was late for his accident.

Split Personality

The man with a split personality is the only one who can go out on a double date by himself.

Spouting

Consider the whale: It never gets into trouble until it comes up and starts spouting.

Statesmen

The best that can be said for some of our statesmen is that they remind us of other statesmen who are worse.

Statistics

Facts are stubborn things, but statistics are more pliable.

Statistician

To a statistician, fractions speak louder than words.

Statues

Statues are erected to the memory of famous people, but they are really for the birds.

Status Symbols

Some people own so many status symbols, they're absolutely in awe of themselves.

Sticky

Even when freshly washed and relieved of all obvious confections, children tend to be sticky.

—*Fran Lebowitz*

Stingy

The stingy man: Money goes through his fingers like glue.

Stocks and Bonds

The best time to buy stocks and bonds is always in the past.

Story

We may be willing to tell a story twice but are never willing to hear it more than once.

—*William Hazlitt*

Straight and Narrow

The straight and narrow path is never congested by heavy traffic.

Stretched

Man's mind stretched to a new idea never goes back to its original dimensions.
—*Oliver Wendell Holmes*

Strike Oil

My formula for success is rise early, work late, and strike oil.
—*J. Paul Getty*

Stubborn

The man who does not think as you do is apt to be stubborn.

Stumbling

One person's stumbling block is another person's stepping-stone.

Stupidity

What people lack in intelligence, they usually make up for in stupidity.

Suburbs

By the time you have finished paying for your home in the suburbs, they are no longer the suburbs.

Subway

The subway has put women on an equal standing with men.

Succeed

All men want to succeed—some want to succeed so badly, they're even willing to work for it.

Success

None of the secrets of success will work unless you do.

* * *

Sometimes it's harder to be a success than to become one.

* * *

You can sum up his success here in one word: *lucky.*

* * *

Nothing recedes like success.

* * *

If at first you do succeed, it's probably your father's business.

*   *   *

Success is only a matter of luck—ask any man who has failed.

*   *   *

There is no shortcut to success; if you want to reach the Promised Land, you must go through the wilderness.

*   *   *

If at first you don't succeed, cry, cry again.

Sudden Wealth

Most people cannot stand sudden wealth, but then most people do not have to.

Suffer

It is easier for a woman to suffer in silence if she knows someone is watching.

Suicide

Life is as you take it, and there are many ways of committing suicide.

Summer

Summer is the season when the air pollution is much warmer.

Superior

Superior men seldom feel superior, and inferior men seldom feel inferior.

Superstitious

You don't have to be superstitious to think it's unlucky to have 13 children.

Suspense

The suspense is terrible; I hope it will last.

—*Oscar Wilde*

Suspicious

Nothing can happen but the suspicious man believes that somebody did it on purpose.

—*Robert Lynd*

Swing Hard

Don't forget to swing hard, in case you hit the ball.

—*Woodie Held*

Tact

Tact is the art of thinking twice before saying nothing.

* * *

Tact: to lie about others as you would have them lie about you.

—*Oliver Herford*

Take-Out

There's a great take-out place in Beverly Hills: Kentucky Fried Pheasant.

Talk

Women eat while they are talking; men talk while they are eating.

—*Malcolm de Chazal*

* * *

People who like to shoot off their mouths never run out of ammunition.

Talker

Many a glib talker has a lot of depth on the surface, but way down deep is very shallow.

Talking

I've just spent an hour talking to her for a few minutes.

Taxes

The reward for saving your money is being able to pay your taxes without borrowing.

Taxpayer

The average taxpayer believes in only one kind of government handout: the kind that takes the government's hand out of his pocket.

Tea

Take a lesson from tea: Its real strength comes out when it gets into hot water.

Teakettle

Remember the teakettle: When it's up to its neck in hot water, it sings.

Teenager

You are never too old to learn, unless you're a teenager.

* * *

When a teenager is watching television, listening to her record player, and talking on the phone, she is probably doing her homework.

Television

Television enables you to be entertained in your home by people you wouldn't have in your home.

—*David Frost*

Temper

Keep your temper—no one else wants it.

Tense

The trouble with most of us is that we are living in the present—tense.

Think

When you stop to think, don't forget to start again.

Thinks

A man can do more than he thinks he can, but he usually does less than he thinks he does.

Three Cars

So far I have paid off three cars: my doctor's, my dentist's, and my shrink's.

Three Principal Things

The three principal things that hold civilization together are the safety pin, the paper clip, and the zipper.

Tickets

There's only one thing more brutal than a football game, and that's the price of the tickets.

Time

Time changes with time: In youth, time marches on; in middle age, time flies; and in old age, time runs out.

* * *

Nothing makes time go so fast as buying on it.

* * *

Time may be a great healer, but it's a lousy beautician.

Time to Be Home

When you're young, your mother tells you what time you have to be home; when you are grown up and married, your babysitter tells you.

Tolerance

The test of courage comes when we are in the minority; the test of tolerance comes when we are in the majority.

—*Ralph W. Sockman*

Tongue

One of the first things you learn when studying a foreign language is that the word *tongue* is feminine.

Toupee

You know you're getting old when your toupee turns gray.

* * *

He's wearing a recycled toupee. If you look very closely, you can see where it used to say "Welcome."

* * *

His toupee makes him look 20 years sillier.

—*Bill Dana*

Travel

Travel is only glamorous in retrospect.

—*Paul Theroux*

Tribute

I feel it is time that I also pay tribute to my four writers, Matthew, Mark, Luke and John.

—*Bishop Fulton J. Sheen*

Trouble

The capacity for getting into trouble and the ability for getting out of it are seldom combined in the same person.

* * *

With me a change of trouble is as good as a vacation.

—*Lloyd George*

* * *

The man who always laughs at his trouble will never have trouble finding things to laugh at.

Troubles

I am an old man and have known a great many troubles, but most of them never happened.

—*Mark Twain*

* * *

When you tell people your troubles, half of them are not interested, and the other half are glad to learn that you're getting what you deserve.

Truth

When in doubt, tell the truth.

—*Mark Twain*

* * *

Teach your child always to tell the truth, but not always to be telling it.

Turbulence

Did you ever realize that serving coffee on an airplane causes turbulence?

Two Kinds of People

There will always be two kinds of people: those who say what they think, and those who keep their friends.

Ulcers

We don't get ulcers from what we eat, but from what's eating us.

Uncle Sam

The reason Uncle Sam has to wear such a tall hat is that he is always passing it around.

Understanding

The best way to keep from stepping on the other fellow's toes is to put yourself in his shoes.

Unexpected Guests

A husband's job is to keep talking to unexpected guests at the front gate while his wife straightens up the living room.

United Nations

The United Nations is a concert of nations with too many wind instruments.

United States

The United States can do anything any other country can do, except borrow money from the United States.

Unpleasant Duty

A person should do one unpleasant duty every day just to keep himself in moral trim.

—*William James*

Use

It is almost as great a misfortune to be of use to everybody as to be of use to nobody.

—*Baltasar Gracian*

Vacation

In planning a vacation, the rule is this: Take along half as much baggage and twice as much money.

Vanity

The only cure for vanity is laughter, and the only fault that's laughable is vanity.

—*Henri Bergson*

Vice President

Once there were two brothers: One ran away to sea, the other was elected vice-president—and nothing was ever heard from either of them again.

—*Thomas R. Marshall*

Virtues

Virtues are learned at mother's knee, vices at some other joint.

Visitors

Fish and visitors smell in three days.

—*Benjamin Franklin*

Wait

The man who has done nothing but wait for his ship to come in has already missed the boat.

Wall Street

The man who butts his head against the stock market soon learns why it is called Wall Street.

War

The worst thing about war is that it seldom kills off the right people.

Washington

Washington is the place where nobody believes a rumor until it has been officially denied.

* * *

Wouldn't it be wonderful if our officials in Washington could solve our money problems the way we keep solving theirs?

Washington is the seat of the government, and the tax-payer is the pants pocket.

Washrooms

Service station washrooms are places where it takes you ten minutes just to clean the soap.

Weaker Sex

The weaker sex is the stronger sex because of the stronger sex's weakness for the weaker sex.

Weather

There are five kinds of weather: spring, summer, fall, winter, and unusual.

Weight

Losing weight is no problem; the trick is to lose it so that it doesn't find its way back.

Well-Adjusted

A well-adjusted person is one who can play golf and bridge as if they were games.

Wheel

Fortunately, the wheel was invented before the car; otherwise, the scraping noise would be terrible.

White Lies

Permit your child to tell white lies, and he will grow up color-blind.

Wicked

The wicked flee when no man pursueth, but they make better time when the sheriff is after them.

Wild Beasts

There are few wild beasts more to be dreaded than a talking man having nothing to say.

—*Jonathan Swift*

Will

The man who makes no will makes lawyers his heirs.

Willing

The world is full of willing people; some willing to work, the rest willing to let them.

—*Robert Frost*

Willpower

Willpower is what makes you do what you have to do when you hate to do it most.

* * *

Willpower is to the mind like a strong blind man who carries on his shoulders a lame man who can see.

—*Schopenhauer*

Wind

It is an ill wind that blows when you leave the hairdresser.

—*Phyllis Diller*

Winter

One of the most popular winter sports is taking a plane to Florida.

Wise

The only men who can solve the world's problems can be found driving taxis.

Wise Guys

Some guys are wise, and some are wise guys.

Wit

A fellow who thinks he's a wit is usually half right.

Woman

As soon as you cannot keep anything from a woman, you love her.

—*Paul Geraldy*

* * *

There are two periods in a man's life when he doesn't understand a woman: before marriage and after marriage.

Woman's Intuition

If a woman's intuition is so reliable, why does she have to ask so many questions?

Women

When an irresistible force meets an immovable object, both women get mad.

* * *

The man who says he can understand women is either a psychiatrist or in need of one.

* * *

Men always study women, and know nothing about them; women never study men, and know all about them.

Words

Man does not live by words alone, despite the fact that sometimes he has to eat them.

—Adlai Stevenson

Work

If you want your ship to come in, you must build a dock.

❋ ❋ ❋

All things come to him who waits, but they come faster if he meets them halfway.

❋ ❋ ❋

Nothing is really work unless you would rather be doing something else.
—*James M. Barrie*

❋ ❋ ❋

Some people find that the hardest time to get any work done is between coffee breaks.

World

The world is a book, and those who do not travel, read only a page.
—*St. Augustine*

Worm

The worm always turns, but he doesn't always give you the signal in advance.

Worry

We probably wouldn't worry about what people think of us if we could know how seldom they do.

Writer

He is a writer for the ages—the ages of four to eight.

—*Dorothy Parker*

Writing

Writing a book is an adventure: It begins as an amusement, then it becomes a mistress, then a master, and finally a tyrant.

—*Winston Churchill*

Wrong

This, it seems to me, is the most severe punishment—finding out you are wrong.

—*Walter Winchell*

Yes and No

Yes and no are the oldest and simplest words, but they require the most thought.

—*Pythagoras*

Youthful Figure

What's the best way to get a youthful figure? Ask a woman her age.

Zoo

A zoo is a place devised for animals to study the habits of human beings.

—*Oliver Herford*

Other Books by Bob Phillips

For more information, send a self-addressed stamped envelope to:

Family Services
P.O. Box 9363
Fresno, California 93702